THE MINDFUL PARENT

THE MINDFUL PARENT

Nurturing Connection and Empathy

MARLOWE SINCLAIR

QuillQuest Publishers

CONTENTS

CHAPTER 1

Introduction to Mindful Parenting

The program we have developed is built on the model of the eight-week mindfulness-based stress reduction program designed by Jon Kabat-Zinn in 1979 at the University of Massachusetts Medical Center. Although the intention of that program was to support individuals in dealing with various types of physical and emotional pain and stress, its principles and practical applications can be of great help to parents. Over the past decade or more, research on mindfulness has burgeoned, and elements of MBSR and similarly based mindfulness programs have been adapted for and successfully implemented in many different settings with diverse populations, such as prisons, hospitals, mental health centers, and large corporations. Many of these adaptations are modified versions to accommodate specific interests, ages, and abilities. Our adaptation of the mindfulness-based stress reduction program draws on and complements all of the others in that it focuses specifically on parents and parenting concerns. We have worked to integrate and weave together a multitude of creative adaptations and ideas into the following mindfulness meditation-practice stress reduction program for parents, entitled the "Mindful Parent."

At its core, mindful parenting is simply about being present with and attentive to your child. Being fully present with awareness and acceptance, even when we don't necessarily like the unfolding moments of our children's lives, can be extraordinarily challenging. When a child is laughing, playing, doing well in school, or just plain happy, such presence and attentiveness isn't usually an issue. However, when we have a stressed-out toddler tantrumming her way through the grocery store or a challenging teenager taking the car without permission, most parents don't like what they see and feel. The general tendency is that we compulsively react to whatever is occurring, often with a limited menu of automatic emotional responses. As parents, we react based on our own thoughts and feelings, and lose the opportunity to respond to our child from a more compassionate, well-thought-out place.

CHAPTER 2

Understanding Connection and Empathy in Parenting

Parents who seek to truly connect with their children, creating both structural and emotional security, are also those who are likely to pay close attention and become more attuned, if not more empathic, as a result of their close connection. They are also more likely to be able to see that their children have psychological or emotional states, let alone physical needs or desires. In closing, creating connection with our children through bonding and boundaries allows them to feel recognized, realized, valued, vibrant, and vital. Only when they have internalized these five components, realizing the single-minded power of interconnection, are they likely to grow into thriving, fully alive humans who also find it easy to connect with others. With their social and emotional intelligence enhanced, they are less likely to become damaged, antisocial, or criminal human beings.

It is a tale as old as human civilization itself. Two million years ago, the first humans gathered around campfires at the end of the day's work. There, people connected through the sharing of food, stories, and experiences. Since time immemorial, our ability to connect with others has been at the core of what it means to be human. Our drive to connect with others is not restricted to Homo sapiens only. With the arrival of children, there is an added imperative: to help them survive and thrive, we must form deep, lasting bonds. Research shows that forging such connections with children enhances intellectual, physical, social, and emotional health. Across time and culture, thriving in children grows from connections with their adult attachment figures. These connection processes hold when adapted for single, multiple, gathered, gay, or step-family configurations.

The Importance of Connection

Connection is the human bond that one person forms with another. It's the ability to form an emotional dialogue - sometimes spoken, sometimes silent - with another human being. It's the understanding that such dialogue is the truest gift of life. The connection that we have with one another is what creates and sustains life. It is the medium through which interaction occurs. Interpersonal connection is what makes life worth living. It is the source of meaning and the foundation of mental health. Human beings are born needing love and connection to ensure the survival of the species. In addition, everyone who has ever lived has experienced moments of connection with another person that have been transformational. These moments encapsulated the human experience in a few shared or exchanged glances, looks, touches, or sounds.

Connection is what comes before anything else can happen. Anything that is going to provide a context for risk-taking. Anything that is ever going to provide the fertile ground of the maturation so many programs try to goad our children into. Connection to the family, connection to the parents, connection to the past, connection to the present, connection to nature, connection to the universe, connection to music, and to their unconscious, whatever it is. That's the big, big job of parents. To provide the context of a warm, responsive, responsible, loving connection. And I think that becomes increasingly difficult in a society that really doesn't have any kind of script or storyline to give parents permission to make that your primary reason for having children at all.

Empathy as a Core Parenting Skill

Empathy is the cornerstone of home life and of healing. It is the essence of good listening skills, ability to operationalize advice and therapeutic change, and is the strength of lasting clinical relationships. Indeed, although the business of parenting often gets more attention than the human interaction and empathy that is at its heart, it is an absence of empathy that is often associated with neglect and abuse of children. Indeed, several forms of emotional abuse, such as chronically responding to a child's emotional needs with negative or punitive responses, is associated with similar changes in the brain (frontal lobe) as those found in physical abuse cases.

Empathy lies at the heart of parenting and in many ways defines it. In caring relationships, both parties matter and the relationship exists because of their shared connection. Not only are connections essential for the very survival of young children - this is how latently and dependently young children come into the world - but they are the currency of relationship. Our relationships, and certainly our closest interpersonal connections, are valuable to the extent that they reflect each other's reality. In this sense, we need the other. We need to be seen, heard, and known. That means valued not for how the other would like us to be, but valued for who we truly are. This ability to be reflective and honoring of the reality of the other is empathy. It is the skill that makes your parenting of another human unique - indeed, the most special work of nurturing and development of which a human is capable.

Principles of Mindful Parenting

Mindful parenting is a natural outgrowth of a daily practice of mindfulness meditation. You respond to your child with a clear mind, an open heart, and habits of compassion and wisdom. Disconnect from our true nature, from our bodies, thoughts, and emotions, or from something larger we might choose to call the Self or Spirit, can result if we become too steeped in life's activities. But by beginning the practice we undertake, we feel the process with our minds and our bodies. When we are relating warmly, responsibly, and openly to our emotions, three ingredients - ease, effectiveness, and non-irritability - are experienced in every cell of our bodies.

Through our personal practices, we discover a way to be present that allows us to become increasingly available to ourselves and our children each moment. We create love by living it, and the narrow bond we have with our child can expand as we devote ourselves to practicing love each day, in both formal and spontaneous ways. We can use simple reminders as cues to help us. If mindful moments like the simple exercises in the section on "The Power of Attention" have resulted in a clear mind or a peaceful moment, give yourself kudos. Notice how this kind of attention flows easily and creates space. Next time, and in between other tasks, remember these mindful moments of peace and clarity and cultivate such states in longer, more formal times alone with yourself.

Presence and Awareness

Like in any area of practice, the key principles of mindfulness can be practically applied to boost our connection with our children. Parents with some awareness of mindfulness are able to observe reality unfolding and develop the habit of being present in the here and now. This can increase sensitivity towards others' needs. Sometimes, our own busyness, or our involvement with our daily concerns, or sometimes just our own dullness or lack of discernment, prevent us from really seeing and connecting with the people around us. I think that if you are interested in loving your children, the beginning point is to observe your child... to have the time to listen, not from the top of your height... not from the bottom of your lack of time and irritation... but the time to listen... to speak... to comfort... to know each other... because loving very much means knowing very much.

As we become parents, the way that we relate to our own inner and outer reality is crucial. To cultivate a peaceful family, it is essential to work with our habitual patterns. The pioneering work on mindful parenting, by Myla and Jon Kabat-Zinn, has inspired others to explore the practice of meditation in the parenting process. Their book, "Everyday Blessings: The Inner Work of Mindful Parenting", is rich with insights, personal anecdotes, and suggestions for practice. They offer an in-depth exploration of key aspects of mindfulness, with a particular emphasis on living with children. Many of the points, particularly in regard to stress and our attitudes, were applicable to interactions with all of the people in our lives, especially children.

Non-judgmental Acceptance

Wholeness according to many wisdom traditions includes negative and positive states of mind, low and high energies, and harsh and soft modes of thinking. Even that which we wish we didn't have is part of an organic whole, from which we cannot simply pluck living tares and toss them into oblivion. Our darker moments are part of who we are: hating them is an act of self-violence, a damaging form of self-estrangement. It's better to incorporate them into an expanded sense of self. Mindfulness interventions that foster non-judgmental acceptance of negative states decrease anxiety and depression. Mindful parents who make no account of children's emotions also reduce the likelihood of a special kind of adolescent psychological maladjustment called avoidant reactivity. The recent literature is telling us that true improvement is better fueled by self-acceptance than by self-criticism. The key motivator for positive change isn't a surge of guilt or self-damnation, but a connection with deeply held values, and a compassionate commitment to pursuing strategies that advance them.

At first, it may not make sense to approach our negative judgments of ourselves with acceptance, or even with non-judgment. After all, we need to change the things in us that need changing, right? It's true that change often enters our lives through criticism - someone else's or our own: "I'm critical of myself because I want to be better." And true enough, we can direct compassion towards the self-critic within us: "I'm critical because I want to change. My heart goes out to the part of me that finds it so hard to stay present. To push yourself to present-centeredness feels impossible at times, doesn't it? My heart goes out to you for all the struggles you have had with your challenging moments." By this means we can respond to self-criticism in mixed fashion, part concern, and part indulgence. But we all encounter parts of ourselves that do not want to change. Parts we wish weren't there in the first place.

Compassion and Kindness

The hearts of children are open. They see the purity and the essence of every human soul, and as they mature, they will understand the importance of celebrating and honoring the human spirit of kindness, compassion, and empathy.

Cultivating compassion by extending love and empathy is a nurtugar has found that it enables us to become more deeply empathetic to those around us. Children are trustworthy guides who know the path of love from the heart. They look at the world with eyes of wonder, their hearts overflow with love and compassion, and they act with an open mind that is free from any preconceptions. Each and every step in their journey is a testament to the faith that we are all interconnected with one another, regardless of religion, skin color, culture, or economics.

Real kindness is not about making ourselves feel better or feel good about what we have done. It is about recognizing the essence of another human being and letting that person know that their pain, struggles, and needs matter to us. To empathize deeply is to cultivate the deep awareness that only healthy interaction with others is beneficial, and that we must care for the people we encounter with love and mutual respect.

Compassion and kindness are manifestations of unconditional love that are fueled by empathy and understanding. They are the force that enables us to reach out toward another with the desire to alleviate suffering. When we are compassionate, we are not invested in the outcome. We hope to help but understand that only each of us can walk our path. We do not judge or criticize other people's actions or ourselves. When we connect to our common humanity and shared suffering, we wish with all our hearts that our pain is relieved.

CHAPTER 4

Mindful Communication with Children

I encourage you to intentionally connect with patience and wakefulness during the time you spend with your children—rather than multitasking, doing two things at once, or rushing through daily activities. When multitasking in a scatterbrained manner, you are not actually with your child during the interaction. These moments of your daily life need not be lost or disregarded moments. They are an excellent opportunity for informal practice—the opportunity to check in with your child is a mindfulness practice. You can bring gentle attentiveness and wholehearted presence to these precious moments of your life. There is no need to feel hurried or pulled in two directions. In cultivating this connection, you have taken your first steps toward parent-child mindfulness. If you ever find that you become swept away in your communication or in any of your interactions with your child, it seems that you have lost touch with them, return your focus to your breath or your sensations as an anchor in the moment. The very practice of returning your attention to the present moment is a fundamental part of mindful communication and of relationship at any age.

Mindful communication with our children can enhance connection and empathy, and plays a significant part in nurturing a strong parent-child relationship. By communicating mindfully, we are giving our children a gift every time they are in our presence. As a parent, you can mindfully attend to your child, physically and emotionally, through mindful listening and expressing both formally and informally with full attention. Be present with your child as you listen, attend to your child's feelings through your words, tone, and body language, and when walking together, sitting together, reading, eating, completing housework, driving, shopping, etc.

Active Listening

Remember, it's about them – not me. Active listening is focusing on what is happening in the moment; it is being present, not checking mental to-do lists at the time. Fully concentrate, understand, respond, and remember. The skills involved in active listening might be simple but the practice is not necessarily easy. The busyness of our minds can easily distract us. A deeper connection with your beloved has evolved when there is an understanding, empathy, and kindness that comes from active listening. In time, this relationship tool helps our beloved feel safe with us to share that which may not be shared with others. Active listening reduces misunderstandings, arguments, and resentment. By not imposing on their thoughts, feelings, or emotions, we are taking the time to let them sort through things for themselves – to be an emotional guide – as they independently resolve a little part of their puzzle. In time, a child who feels listened to will grow to be an adult who really can listen.

Active listening is the process of genuinely hearing and understanding another person's feelings and thoughts. It is a skill – one that can be developed, practiced, and improved if we set our intention to listen to understand rather than to respond. As parents, active listening can pave the way to a more intimate and harmonious way of communicating with our children and model an important skill for life. Being human, we naturally want to make things better, and in our attempts to soothe our child's upset, we may tend to say things such as, "It's OK. You're fine," or "Here, have a cookie. You'll feel better." There are times when a distraction technique is appropriate, yet deep down inside, our children may be longing to be understood, to be heard, and to not be brushed aside too quickly. We all want to be heard, and our children are no different. Real listening is a fundamental skill to ensure a deep connection. It plays an essential part in parenting, whether your child is an infant, toddler, preschooler, in kindergarten, primary, high, or even college.

Empathetic Responses

In some cases, it is helpful to talk about why she is so upset. Doing so will help her to understand her feelings and to gain some perspective. You won't be able to help her sort through her feelings if you can't stay calm yourself. Remind yourself that moments like these are opportunities to connect, to help your child learn to manage emotions, and to recover from stress. Coach her to calm down, such as by taking deep breaths. Then talk about what she can do and how she can solve the problem. I might cheerfully say, "Come on, let's come up with a solution. What if we set up the picnic in the dining room and open the shades wide? We can pretend we are surrounded by trees and flowers until it is really nice enough to eat outside."

One of the first steps in responding with empathy to our child's strong emotions is to carefully listen so that we can say, "You sound really upset." Let your child know that you understand why she is upset. "You're disappointed that we can't eat dinner outside tonight. You were looking forward to playing in the yard after you ate." Validate her feelings: "Anyone would be upset when they hear that something they were looking forward to might not happen." She needs you to help her acknowledge that she is distressed before she can calm down.

CHAPTER 5

Cultivating Self-Compassion as a Parent

To develop self-compassion, it is essential to halt the automatic pilot and to pause and breathe deeply to find our emotional center when we notice an emotional upset. Without practice, we only have the opportunity to reflect after our response, during the time when our misguided interactions are pointed out to us or when we notice their negative effects. Creating intentional breathing spaces at specific places during the day creates the focused attention to notice our strong feelings when they arise. This practice of compassionate response can also bring us the time we need to move our energies and responses away from reactivity and toward connection and warmth in our interactions with others.

Stanford and Neff both speak to the idea that "the more we suppress and deny painful experiences, the more those experiences control us," thereby taking over how we interact with our children. When we are lost in anger and reactivity, we tend to pass along negative messages to our children, release stress hormones that have a negative impact on both our body and our long-term parenting, and affect everybody else around us. The idea of healthy emotional regulation is to hold the difficult feelings with honor and respect for having been generated through suffering and provide the soothing they need in order to transform. Providing this holding and soothing is seen as self-compassion. Self-compassion allows us to meet suffering and difficult emotions with kindness rather than being overrun by them and reacting.

CHAPTER 6

Practicing Mindfulness in Daily Parenting Activities

In this section, we present three chapters on how to let people try. In each chapter, we will continue to present the information related to each training session, facilitating participation, the purpose of that session, the purpose, the main principles, the stages in which each training session will focus on the focus, how to work on deepening learning through the mindfulness exercises-practice included in that chapter. Each of you should feel free to include short breaks in informal mindfulness exercises in the activities of daily life. These can be as complex or as basic as you wish. As a facilitator, your role is to guide individuals towards a better understanding of mindfulness. After reading this manual, we suggested that simpler approaches focus on non-formal activities, tasks, family, and professional life situations. Mindfulness sessions are a way of allowing participants to experience mindfulness in action. Simply put, practicing formal mindfulness exercises not only to train this quality of presence but also to realize the extent to which mindfulness is required. It covers all aspects of life, including daily routines such as having lunch, taking notes, or doing small chores/tasks around the house.

In this session, parents were encouraged to take an informal approach to mindfulness, simply paying attention with friendliness from moment to moment. Mindfulness was brought into activities that are performed in a person's daily life. It is interesting to see how people react when they realize that when they focus most of their attention on their present experience, their lives are more satisfying, and they succeed in relating to their surroundings in a more understanding and connected way. Despite the fact that everyone thought they did, the fact is that several people tend to spend a considerable part of their day worrying about the future or getting entangled by past events and regretting them. The community got involved in various activities focused on developing the mindfulness that was incorporated as small exercises into non-formal daily activities. Participants were encouraged to use their breath in their daily activities to help them feel more unified, more present. Some people do not know, but the breath is a great ally when practicing mindfulness, by also serving as a focal point to move that attention and to be attentive to any moments in their day. Participants were encouraged to make regular pauses to review their intentions, to act more compassionately, and to return to the present moment. They were also encouraged to pay more attention to the people around them, to listen more, to notice emotions, and to perceive feelings in their physical bodies. Mindful community participants knew that developing these capacities as a habit was a challenge and that it required training and persistence.

Mealtime

Young children eat little and often and should eat with the family whenever possible. Eating three huge meals puts pressure on the newly birthed digestive system, leads to overeating, and can contribute to gastric reflux, colic, and poor sleep. Eating with you means that babies, toddlers, and young children are more likely to eat fruits, vegetables, and protein instead of an unbalanced diet of low-nutrient refined carbohydrates, sugar, and trans fat, which can set unhealthy eating habits for life and contribute to many health problems. I'm passionate about family mealtime: you and your child need to eat anyway, so why not do it together in a conscious atmosphere that calms the mind and nurtures the spirit of all participants? Also, children are not born knowing how to eat; mealtime is an opportunity to model and learn healthy dining manners, which are essential as your child grows and begins to eat with family and friends. Early proper nutrition helps create a healthy body and brain, and healthy meals tell your child that you care about and respect her body. As your child grows, she is much less likely to eat meals made with wholesome, pesticide-free, seasonal, organic food if they've watched you eat McDonald's while text-messaging. And what tales your child could tell her friends about the gooey fruit, ugli fruit, and fresh pastas she's adventurously tried in the nurturing environment of her home!

Mealtimes provide an opportunity to look at our children, connect, and model healthy, conscious nutrition ourselves. Each meal you eat with your children gives you a chance to share yourself with them. This time can give them the experience of laughing, storytelling, sharing, and quiet mindful mutual focus that will shape their memories and relationship to you and themselves. Mealtime can easily turn into a battleground, an entertaining free-for-all, or time during which everyone except the cook zones out with TV and cellular devices. On days I don't spend with Elin and her boys, I look forward to cooking a simple, nutritious supper, going to dinner with a mindful attitude, and using the time to unwind from my day with El and then talk about everything Elin and I want to discuss.

The intimacy and relaxation we all enjoy let us enter our separate evenings replete and grounded.

Bedtime Routine

Relax the bedtime routine: Take the time to be present with your child and put him to bed with a joyful heart instead of hurrying. Too often bedtime rituals are rushed and the child ends up feeling neglected at the end of the day. They want to feel loved and important. They love having a story, hearing a joke, or learning a new word. This also gives them the closeness they need after feeling "abandoned" during the day when we were tending to our responsibilities. Set a special time aside for each of your children: They each want your attention for themselves. Give them this special moment individually. Even if it is for just ten minutes, they will remember it and look forward to it. Most importantly, they will feel very special.

This may well be the most important routine in a parent's day. A child who gets a good night's sleep will be better able to handle stress during the day and will be a happier, more cooperative child who can make more positive decisions. What's more, this is the time when there is enough silence and intimacy to have a conversation with your child. Telling a story, reading a book, saying good night—these are all meaningful ways to connect with your child.

CHAPTER 7

Building Resilience in Children through Mindful Parenting

Mindful precepts and related practices pave the way as our children's underlying styles of effective learning while enhancing effective parent help and effectiveness. Between our children's milestone behavioral and brain development phases, an interval lost on our past generations, we can highlight mindfulness milestones on the power surge of intentional learning that captivates these special development periods and thoughtful parent practices that weave them. This is a special urgently rapid period where parents can enhance and savor being guided and confided in. Building resilience is especially important during these milestone development and reflective milestone discussions. Mindful parenting is important. Mindful precepts and mindful stay in addition to stay and play generations are prime guides to optimal child development.

Parenting today is beset with parental concerns on 'overdoing it,' being way too indulgent, constantly checking our children on performance measures, helicopter parenting, or overpermissive styles, and excessive hovering and indulging. Given poor media influences, exposure to other role models, and sometimes self-doubts and a sense of perfectionism or hopes to spare children from hardship and injury, mindful parenting becomes all the more important. Here we list those practices that are especially beneficial and empowering for children. From their intensive behavioral and brain development to self-discovery, mastery, and self-reflective learning milestones, each of these practices can seem very difficult and challenging as a 'parental task,' as to why not do them another day. Mindfulness requires priming and knowing one's needs, vulnerabilities, and strong controlling patterns.

CHAPTER 8

Mindful Discipline and Setting Boundaries

The lack of interest in applying "discipline" techniques, and confusion about how or when to do so, is a common theme in my work with parents. There is no one-size-fits-all recipe for handling conflicts and difficult times. The good news is there are a few basic principles that, with practice, can lead you to the solution that will work for you: Follow your heart and know what you want. There is no joy in being angry; it is an uncomfortable and unfamiliar place for your being. Nevertheless, your anger, or more specifically, your response to your anger, can actually help you. The wise course is to maintain awareness of your feelings, staying open to what might emerge, blessing and transforming your feelings of anger instead of allowing anger to consume you - and finally, to take appropriate action.

Thoughtfully setting and administering rules and consequences is an integral part of the mindful parenting journey. When we take appropriate action in response to our children's actions - and do so mindfully and in the service of growth, rather than simply out of anger or a wish for revenge - we help our children learn, and of equal importance, develop a sense of accountability and compassionate responsibility. Whether your children are toddlers, tweens, or teens, it is never too late to become, or to embody, the mindful parent. All your children really want is for you to show up. Every step you take on this path strengthens the empathic relationship with yourself and your children, transforming both self and other in ways that shape and alter the future.

CHAPTER 9

Balancing Self-Care and Parenting Responsibilities

Women often feel secondary to men. Consequently, they may become their own worst enemies when it comes to self-care issues. One of the most important resources is to take time alone. While the day is filled with making meals for others, packing lunches, delivering them from place to place, helping with homework, talking on the phone, going to the dentist, food shopping, nurse-maiding a petitioner, is the women's day filled with quiet time for herself. No satisfied being alone. No moments when the sun is descending outside and you are watching a portion of the news, sitting out on the deck with a snack. Few women are able to take time alone, because taking time alone in our society is one of the five most taboo, threatening needs, for which many women feel guilty and for which society offers the least support.

Work-life balance may not be just a luxury but actually a survival skill. This means doing what it takes to bring more balance to your life. In many two-parent families, women feel more of the ongoing pressure to take care of children, family, and household needs. Mothers sometimes feel torn trying to balance the conflicting demands of work and family. I consider it crucial for both parents to help children feel safe and secure. You need to take care of yourself in order to take the best care of others. Notice how often when we do something for ourselves it feels like indulgence, rather than necessary sustenance. It is interesting to notice the potty session, in contrast, where we relieve ourselves without thinking it indulgence.

Mindful Parenting in Challenging Situations

Rather than approaching situations that make us crazy with a magic wand – getting rid of them through some unrealistic escape – we can offer a second, more realistic method of dealing mindfully with those challenging times when our stress factor becomes overbearing. The process of finding those special quiet times can nurture a patient and compassionate self, who can then parent with greater respect and attentiveness. In the following section, we offer several vignettes of particularly challenging situations. Then, chapter by chapter, we explore specific ideas for mindful responses to a variety of stressful moments through the encouragement of options to the reactivity muscle reply to which we have become too accustomed.

As parents, we fantasize that with mindfulness we will never lose our cool, always have good multitasking energy, fit the ideal of the good parent, and never become impatient with repetitive questions, squabbling siblings, or messy rooms. Perhaps if we had become a circus clown, we could find an outlet for that creativity in kinetic nonstop shop, but we chose parenthood at least at this time of our lives. Part of mindful parenting is accepting our fatigue, our need for diversion from the security of constant routine and quiet – knowing that when we take a short walk ourselves, put our feet up and take five deep breaths, or call a friend, we are actually storing up the energy we need both to appreciate the fullness of our lives and to respond appropriately to the myriad challenging situations that arise when we are working to rear our children.

Dealing with Tantrums

Label emotions your child demonstrates: That's your angry face! You feel so upset you're kicking and screaming. Clearly describing feelings may help relieve them. "Talking about difficult feelings can do this by helping children shift from a reactive, emotional, right-brain state to a more logical, left-brain state." Stating strong emotions without judgment, she says, can help children feel that their emotions are accepted, and no behavior is necessary in response. Be sure to mindfully communicate physically as well. Hugs, holding hands, or sitting next to an upset child can communicate an abundance of warmth and affection. "Children also need physical comfort when they are emotionally upset," our therapist friend agrees.

All of us get overwhelmed. None of us – or our children – are perfect. Regardless of the amount of effort you invest in mindfulness practice or parenting, there will be times when everyone simply has a bad morning, afternoon, or day. Allowing yourself the grace and compassion to acknowledge and accept that fact can make it easier to hold out the same grace and compassion for your kids when their inevitable meltdowns occur. No matter how much your child may be acting out, remember that his or her primary need is to sense your warmth and support.

Parenting Through Divorce or Separation

Listening to your child and truly hearing what they have to say, with a deep sense of empathy, is even more important now. It's often difficult for the ego to let go of the fact that your child may prefer living with one parent over the other. It's important to make sure that the parent they don't live with is perceived as a positive source of stability and that kids remain close and attached to that parent also. If kids can feel comfortable living in both homes, it goes a long way to normalizing their lives. They can also feel as if they belong and aren't lost in the shuffle. Provide deep safety by creating a respectful co-parenting relationship. Keep your kids out of adult business and never, ever use them to deliver messages that imply judgment or blame. Hold them close and try praying for your soon-to-be ex. This doesn't have to be a religious act but rather an opportunity to show that you are extending good wishes for their happiness in the world – however you choose to define that happiness.

This transition sometimes means being more connected and empathetic with yourself as a parent. Remembering that your children have the right to maintain a relationship with both parents can be a powerful and often painful, at first, reality. In our book, "The Mindful Divorce," I talk about not seeing myself as a divorced parent, but rather one who loved my kids well and set out to nurture a respectful and co-existent relationship between their father and me. Reframing it like this was empowering and helped make transitions easier for everyone. No matter what your current relationship is with your soon-to-be ex, honor the connection they have with your child when you talk about them or when you communicate with them in the presence of your child.

CHAPTER 11

Cultivating a Mindful Family Environment

Include the family pets as part of the family's environment and care for them accordingly. All this evidence, both scientific and anecdotal, indicates that environment plays a huge role in the happiness of pets and, in addition, that genuine relationships are possible between people and animals. Children who are allowed responsibly to care for pets can experience the joy and empathy that come with the opportunity. Whether your home was created for the sake of children or whether children share a portion of your existence as a result of your desire for a home, you can shape your environment to enhance your family's overall well-being. As you do so, you will be teaching your children about the connection between happiness, gratitude, and the world that surrounds them.

The atmosphere in which a family lives affects each family member for better or for worse. This atmosphere includes both the emotional tenor of family life and the physical environment in which it occurs. The way you maintain your home, the activities you engage in together, and the people and pets you choose to include all contribute to the health and happiness of the relationship among the members of the family. By becoming more mindful of the family's atmosphere, you can both contribute to it more consciously and enjoy it more fully. Various rituals can mark the passing of time and lend meaning to life together. Regular family meetings can give everyone a voice and teach important skills for cooperation and leadership.

Creating Rituals and Traditions

In healthy and vital families, rituals connect the old and the young. They are reference points that can be revisited and reinterpreted in differing shades as developing minds grow and explore the current world in new ways. Family rituals have taken a hit in recent years as our contemporary society eschews that which cannot be done quickly in pursuit of other valued activities or in response to stressful demands. The result, however, is that children grow up isolated from reverence and family coherence, missing the supportive continuum that only tradition can offer across generations. Rituals ground children and help to keep them on a safe path - a valuable leg up in an adult world.

Rituals and traditions are touchstones for families. They bind, connect, and comfort us. They offer life-enhancing rhythms and structure. They can also help group members move through painful and difficult experiences with more grace and resilience - acting as buffers against the vicissitudes of life. By their very nature, they often take the form of repetitive actions that foster the lost art of simple presence. To be present to our family members is the very expression of mindfulness and connection.

Incorporating Mindfulness Practices Together

When viewing our responsibility for our abilities as a portion of a collective whole, it helps model what we wish to influence. The concept of sovereignty can give us a vision for the type of people and parents we strive to be. By feeling help with the day-to-day challenges that parenting offers, it allows us to view this parenting process as part of conquering the personal and global dilemma that we face. Such insight can be empowering at times of personal doubt or societal defeat. With care, empathy, gratitude, and clear visualization, we can be the activists of today, tomorrow, introspectively, and with our children and ultimately others.

Caring adults in support of this growth process are powerful allies, and it is positive when we emphasize the importance of empathy and mutual understanding in our statements. However, the duty lies in attempting to balance this description with a practical understanding of the world our offspring lives in. Research shows that starting our work towards overt (activist) compassion with an understanding of self has a positive effect for the collective we wish to influence. Activist parenting commences at the personal level. We do not need to change every facet of ourselves to become conscientious and caring citizens, but we do need to start this process at the point where it counts the most. If we need to strengthen patience, kindness, or understanding, we can do this through mindful meditation.

CHAPTER 12

The Benefits of Mindful Parenting for Children and Parents

Mindfulness requires that parents become referees and spectators in the challenging game of understanding and interpreting their child's behavior so that they can remain in tune with the child's internal world. Through this ability to respond rather than react, mindful parenting not only enhances an awareness of one's consciousness, but also, in doing so, aids in releasing the attachment fears, emotional dysfunctions, developmental blockages, and psychosomatic illnesses that can occur. Embodying mindful awareness to one's parenting can provide a potent and gentle buffering effect that supports and empowers the family as a whole. With clearer channels of communication and increased empathy, the experience of togetherness will be deepened in a stable family structure. Mindful parenting realizes love indivisibly, and in so doing it is the basis of the newly arising relationship between parents and their offspring and between children and their parents.

We have examined how mindful parenting manifests in practice and discussed the research evidence supporting the benefits of this approach. It would certainly be unfortunate if, however, the only reason for adopting a mindful approach to parenting was to gain a social or moral advantage, or to boost our wellbeing and contentment. Nevertheless, although these can be welcome additional outcomes, for many of us, they are certainly not our first priority. We are involved with children through family structures that require a huge sacrifice of time, energy, and freedom. At the heart of parenting then is not only the frequency of altruistic acts of devotion but also the reciprocity of love.

CHAPTER 13

Overcoming Common Challenges in Mindful Parenting

It is well-known in office? What has been helpful in overcoming these challenges? Due to the cut-off of the mindful attitude. In all these instances, one's mindfulness helps them see how they want to approach the situation and take care of the situation cyclically while seeing their impulses but not have to act on them. When under certain circumstances, when under a high level of stress, mindfulness may be the last thing to apply. What times like that are you likely to not be so mindful? Are the content of the tiff? What has been helpful to gain a level of mindfulness? Keep a file with your thoughts on these subjects while any of you or your partner are challenged by your parents.

You have now read extensively about mindful parenting. It has wonderful benefits for both you and your child, but also presents significant study challenges. Children or circumstances can invite you to react in a way that is the opposite of mindful, but mindful parenting is contagious in a positive way. The more you use it, the more others learn from it and are inclined to practice it. You are courageous to pursue a pro-child approach to parenting during times that continually stretch and challenge us. Use the compassion and empathy you practice to make mistakes kindly for yourself, then move forward.

CHAPTER 14

Resources for Further Learning and Support

Aha Parenting

Offering discussions and articles about parenting, Aha Parenting offers perspective, resources, and tips for cultivating emotional health. They also provide parenting support for families looking for information and guidance on raising their children.

Arlene Ramer – Connective Parenting

Arlene Ramer's website offers materials, services, and support for parents to help them parent more effectively and build a closer, stronger relationship with their children.

Center for Nonviolent Communication

The Center for Nonviolent Communication focuses on developing effective, respectful, and compassionate communication, and creating social structures that allow people to respond to others and thrive.

Celebrate Connection

This website is focused on promoting the message of strong parent-child relationships through conscious, present, and compassionate connections. It offers resources and products for baby and parent comfort, as well as nurturing connection and empathy through art and workshops.

Children's Heart Link Ministries

With a heart specifically tuned to healing through connection, Children's Heart Link Ministries provides support, education, and resources for families of children with developmental or regulatory challenges. They specialize in FASD or prenatal alcohol exposure issues, early trauma, attachment challenges, and more.

The Circle of Security

The Circle of Security is a unique relationship-based early intervention program designed to enhance attachment security between parents and their children. The company represents an effort to help parents and professionals worldwide better understand and respond to children's needs.

Conscious Discipline

This company provides education about brain-based and connected products that foster home and school communication. Conscious Discipline focuses on social and emotional learning, discipline, and self-reflection to foster healthy connections.